what we leave behind

by katherine j zumpano

Copyright: Katherine J Zumpano, 2026

All rights reserved. No parts of this book may be used, performed, or reproduced in any manner whatsoever without written permission from the author, except in the case of brief quotations used in reviews or critical articles.

The author expressly prohibits the use of this book for the purposes of training AI models to generate text, including—but not limited to—AI technologies capable of generating works in the same style or genre as this book. No generative artificial intelligence (AI) was used in the writing, creation, or publication of this book.

First Edition
ISBN: 979-8-9947292-0-5

Cover design by Katherine J Zumpano
Interior layout by Katherine J Zumpano

Type set in Georgia

what we leave behind

by katherine j zumpano

for Dad.

TABLE OF CONTENTS

home(town)	9
four	10
my father's daughter	11
first memory	12
on feeling lightning	13
the farm	14
blood	15
ten	16
what we leave behind	17
sisterhood	18
the mountain is out	20
self-portrait as a sapling	21
slug repellent	22
twelve	23
things I'm afraid I'll forget with age	24
wildfire	26
ink	27
168	28
eldest daughter	31
seventeen	32
how to disappear	33
192	34
summer vacation	35
anhedonia	37
late june	38
twenty-one	39
the ache that turned into art	40
when I long for you, I long for sundays	41
I wrote this poem as an offering	43
rootbound	44
in which I compose a love letter	45

twenty-three	46
homecoming	47
empty nest	49
autumnal shift	51
eyes on minneapolis	52
bloodlines *(with sydnee smith)*	54
twenty-four	57
pandemic poem for my mother	58
drop	59
elegy for an unborn daughter	61
strange survivor's guilt	62
the summer joel miller died	63
twenty-six	66
unofficial list of grievances	67
willow	69
denali	70
snowfall	72
on seeing the aurora borealis	74
twenty-seven	75
elegies for a small town	76
return to olympus	81
girlhood	82
trillium falls	83
driving past ghosts *[after Noah Kahan's "The View Between Villages (Extended)"]*	84
thirty	85

home(town)

I don't know how to answer when you ask about my hometown. my life: lived in prolonged pauses between cities, back and forth across the northern border. I came of age waiting, waiting for the next thing. you ask, *where are you from*? I wonder what you mean. where I was born to a frozen february morning? minnesota. where I learned to ride a bike, scuffed knees in a public-school parking lot? ontario. where I met my best friend, feasting on girlhood with a side of midnight snacks? california. where I cried over high school crushes, too much skin and bones and angst? british columbia. where I fell in love with lakes and evergreens and him? washington. where I'll go next? I don't know yet. life lived in motion isn't easy to stop.

home: every town in
which roots I put down remain.
everywhere at once.

four

home is a two-bedroom apartment in hennepin county,
and my bedroom looks like the hundred-acre-wood,
and I have a lite brite and a tiny tea set
and dad is teaching me to read and I'm pretty good at it,
and one day I will read all by myself.
there is little to worry about at four, aside from
when dad will take me to the park next
to watch the turtles sunning themselves and diving
into the pond, red shells and soft underbellies, and one time
dad saw a duck trapped in plastic-soda-can-rings,
and turned us around to get scissors to save the duck.
before bed, we play board games or read
(or sometimes we do both) (and sometimes mom joins).
and dad sings me the beatles, sings me a lullaby—
good night, sleep tight—
and when I am older, I will have forgotten so much
about what it is like to be four, to be learning
to tie my shoes and write, to be learning the world.
but I will not forget this: dad's voice singing gently
in the nightlight-lit room, singing me to sleep.
good night, sleep tight.

my father's daughter

my father has never been good
at delivering bad news, sharing it
      uncomfortably—
              abruptly—
and so I never learned to give bad news either.
so much of my father lives in myself:
an affinity for sad, indie films
and sad, indie music; integrity
and a strong moral compass;
humor as a coping mechanism;
humor as a talent; my love of words,
of reading good books and many books
and writing poetry, fostered gently
over thirty years, the greatest gift he has given me.
I lie awake some nights and wonder
what he wanted for me,
if he gazed at me in infancy
with hopes and dreams for my life,
whether I live up to them.
another thing I inherited from my father:
a love of structure, of scheduled routine.
did he have a plan for my life?
did I follow it? if I strayed from his path,
I hope the parts of him living in me led me back,
shaped me into a daughter to be proud of.

first memory

in my first memory, I meet my mother: shy & half-asleep, colors muted from minnesota-winter-morning-dark; her voice, as soft and warm as the california sun; my father's smile at our introduction. a brief series of images radiating coziness—a child's fabrication of something they want to remember, I think. years later, I ask my mother about the day we first met. her memory parallels mine perfectly. my first memory as if by destiny.

on feeling lightning

I am twenty-three / standing in the rain of a pacific northwest thunderstorm on a september midnight / standing at the foot of the stairs in an alley / dim and drenched, potholes turned to puddles / we are worlds away from our cozy candlelit room / we rushed outside at the first crack of thunder / hastily dressed / socks soaked through canvas shoes / jeans plastered to skin / torrential tears, rain on my cheeks / the storm in my bones / energy crackles around me / fine hairs on my arms stand on edge / I am on edge / waiting / my boyfriend pulls me into the garage / into safety / he says *you shouldn't stand out there, it's dangerous under the powerlines* / I don't care / I read somewhere that lightning is hotter than the surface of the sun / I wonder if that's true / I wonder if I could feel the heat on my face if I got close enough / I kiss him in reply / return to the rain, to the risk / normally I am cautious / I never climbed trees or jumped into lakes / I triple-check the door when I leave the house / walk with keys between my knuckles in dark parking lots / compelling curiosity / I wait beneath the powerlines for the lightning / I haven't seen a storm like this in a decade / for a moment I am eleven years old again / playing in the rain of a midwest thunderstorm on a july afternoon / playing in the alley behind my grandparents' house / a memory I had forgotten / revived by a thunderstorm / I want that spark back / I want to feel the lightning, so / I wait / above, the black sky growls / thunder reverberates through me / a pause   and then / the purple sky cracks open / canvas ripped apart by blinding light / in that moment, I swear I am ablaze

the farm

my grandfather's parents owned forty acres of land
in wisconsin. we'd drive across the state
line to visit the farm. beyond cornfields,
green hills rolled across cerulean skies;
to the right stretched a forest,
home to deer & ticks & a black bear I never saw.
my grandfather grew up in a white farmhouse
at the property's edge, knew each creak in the floor
like the back of his hand. in the empty barn,
I imagined pigs & cows & chickens in the stalls;
the silo always bare, too, ferns sprouting from dirt.
what I loved most: the brilliance of the stars—
a promise of tomorrow, a whisper of acceptance.
there are no stars like that in the twin cities, nor any city
I have called home. a city keeps them hidden.
on the farm, there is nothing to drown them out.

I return in my mind; I cannot return to the land,
for I am not of its blood. didn't you know?
a monarchy crumbles without the bloodline
inheriting the castle.
and so memories of childhood are poisoned
and rejection stings until anger until acceptance until
I don't care anyway. I share no blood
with my grandfather, who married my father's mother.
he loves me as his own granddaughter, he always has.
I still walk the farm, gaze at stars above
in my mind's eye—that is good enough for me.

blood

I share no blood with my mother,
but she loves me as her daughter.
an impossibility: a life without her,
in which I am still myself.

an impossibility: in photos, my smile
is a mirror of her sister's. before he passed,
her uncle told me, *I've loved you
from the moment you joined this family.*

I fill out new patient paperwork
with her medical history. later,
in the exam room, I tell the doctor,
you can ignore that. I'm sorry.

any diagnosis would be coincidence.
I tell my mother this over drinks
and she laughs, tells me she forgets, too.
my blood, transfused through love.

ten

home is our first house
on glenfield, and ten is too old
to be carried inside when I fall asleep
in the car. I am growing up,
so I have to be responsible.
I have a little sister and a little brother,
and I clean my own room.
I learn how to ride a bike
and I read at a seventh grade level,
even though I am only in fifth grade.
but ten is still young enough
for childish things.
I know monsters aren't real, but I still
run with the lights off and have nightmares
about the basement.
my friends and I play SPIES at recess,
or sometimes PRINCESSES, or sometimes
tag with the boys.
the boys say they run faster, but that
isn't true—I run faster
than some of them, even in a skirt.
someday I will grow up, and I won't play
pretend or be afraid of monsters
or spend afternoons at the park
or go sledding when it snows.
will I still have fun? will I still laugh,
still smile? I don't know
if adults are just too busy
or if they forget, but I promise myself
I will never forget how to have fun.

what we leave behind

my mother found photographs beneath the refrigerator
in our first house. I wondered
how they were lost, why no one noticed
they were gone or knocked on the door to ask for them.
maybe they fell from the fridge, dropped
by a weak magnet. maybe
they were stored in a box above, stuffed so full
of memories that a few escaped. maybe
they belonged to the house; taken to remember
them by. to remember in case they forget. I have not
forgotten.

I wonder what I have left behind: a bobby pin blending
into carpet / a chip in the paint / an earring back / flecks
of nail polish / the sense of knowing
who I was and what I wanted

sisterhood

my sister brings me flowers
on my twenty-sixth birthday,
a bouquet of white lilies
I arrange in a glass vase to
display on a shelf. I find myself
admiring the lilies often,
thinking of her: of the first time
I held her, crying and
so small, at the hospital;
of whispering across twin beds
in sweltering summer heat; of
games played as children
and sweaters borrowed
unapproved; of her first day
of college, the doubt
in her eyes when we met
for lunch; of her kindness,
always in awe of it.
I think I have learned more
from her than she has from me.

we've always been different.
pick a cliché: oil & water / night
& day / apples & oranges.
sometimes like strangers—but
she has taught me confidence,
how to be myself
without remorse, how to take up   space
and live a life that is full.
my sister brings me flowers
for my birthday and stays for cake,
but the real gift is sisterhood.

for all her life, I have had
the pleasure of watching her grow
into adulthood,
into her beautiful soul.

the mountain is out

spring arrives with rainstorms and signs of life
return to the valley. vibrant yellow daffodils
and fields of tulips in red, orange, purple;
cherry blossoms and pacific dogwoods bloom;
the mountain is out on clear days.
have you listened to the mountains lately?
they will speak if you're willing to listen,
and not just the ones in washington—
every mountain has a story to tell.
they will give you their names,
their true names: kulshan, tahoma,
denali, sultana, tumanguya, agiocochook.
they will tell legends of their beginnings,
epic folklore full of beauty and power.
they will tell you of atrocities witnessed,
of flora & fauna decimated.
they have seen the best and worst
of humanity over millenia,
have been subjugated and renamed
and have not broken. don't you want to learn this?
if you are willing to listen, they will speak.
on clear spring days, when the mountain is out
in the valley, I listen.

self-portrait as a sapling

I knew growing up that I was a sapling planted in the wrong soil, offered to someone without the knowledge or inclination to care for me. my growth at risk, I was given to another. while tended to with love and care, my roots rebelled against the soil, against the new garden. I didn't trust this new gardener. what if I was abandoned, poisoned by the soil in which my roots were replanted, left to rot while the saplings around me thrived? I grew, as all things do, but my growth was stunted, sabotaged by fear. my leaves burst from their buds, faded and colorless. my vines grew short and leggy, skeletal limbs extending towards the sky, fragile. I kept up the illusion of growth while I starved.

the gardener didn't give up. she showed me the same care as the other saplings in the garden. she watered me regularly. she provided her own light when the sun was not enough. she taught me not to fear the rain. she pruned my wilted leaves. she poured her strength into me so I could grow, patient and forgiving and loving. once I accepted love, I began to thrive in the garden. my roots, once fearful of overcrowding, stretched out to touch others. my limbs grew strong, my leaves vibrant. I let the gardener nurture me and felt something I hadn't felt before: safe. if the gardener had given up, I may not have survived. but she never did. she kept trying, strived to keep me alive—and she did. once I accepted her love, I grew into a beautiful thing, into myself.

slug repellent

I visit home for the first time in eleven months
and my brother shows me his garden: cherry tomatoes
and radishes, parsley and fennel.
slugs keep eating the radishes, he says,
        so we research ways to repel slugs. we wrap wire
        around the raised garden bed; we sprinkle
        crushed eggshells over the soil; still the slugs come,
        each radish my brother picks from the ground
        half-eaten and covered in slime. we don't give up.

we research more methods for homemade slug repellent.
we fill a red solo cup with beer, bury it in the dirt,
cover the top with foil. the next morning,
we check our trap and find seven drowned slugs
in the cup. the radishes are finally safe,
thanks to a can of IPA and a gardening blog.
the next time I visit—much sooner
than the last—my brother hands me a radish,
slime-free and untouched.
I don't like radishes, but I savor the crunch.
it means I am home.

twelve

home is with my grandparents at 168
and at twelve, I learn to smack a tetherball
on the same school playground as my mother,
who gets me ready for my first school dance,
wearing braces and a department-store-dress.
my father repeats times tables; he recommends books
about hobbits and mockingbirds, first wives
locked in attics, mice and men.
I share a room with my sister; we have orange
and teal bedsheets and a boxy TV and bins of toys
I am beginning to outgrow. we are growing up,
all of us: my sister starts school, my brother starts talking;
when I bleed through my pajamas,
one grandmother helps wash my sheets;
the other is offended by my body hair.
my best friend lives down the street and
I walk to her house for summer sleepovers, midnight
hot pockets and famous-youtuber-dreams.
we are young enough to hold court
on the kickball field, ~~ketchup~~ blood-stained tissues
on the evidence table; we are old enough
for training bras and crushes on boys.
in notebooks, I start writing novels and song lyrics
and poetry that I don't yet understand.
I am on the precipice, teetering between
childhood and adolescence, at the beginning
of the rest of my life.

things I'm afraid I'll forget with age

my childhood tea set, delicate white porcelain
stored in a wicker basket lined in red gingham;
the floorplan of every home I have ever lived in,
where each room was and the color of the wood
in the kitchens and what I could see
from each bedroom window; the lush greenery
before my uncle moved, emptying the side yard
of bonsai trees; midwestern summers
with my grandparents and cousins, the laughter
of those years; my first published poem;
why I no longer drink wine;
the warmth of my grandmother's eyes;
every story I have ever been told
by all of the people I love
who are no longer here to tell them;
the care with which my honorary uncle crafted a list
of everywhere to go before my first trip to boston;
how the california sun reflects
off the water, off my aunt's eyes, on the wharf,
melts the tension from her bones
in her happiest place on earth; the curves
and loops of my mother's handwriting;
the name of every book and every album
and every film my father has ever recommended;
the name of every friend I have ever loved,
from kindergarten to adulthood; when my niece,
aged six and careful with feelings,
held me close and whispered, *you're my favorite tia*;
the freedom of barefoot summer afternoons;
my first earthquake; my grandfather's laugh;
the day spent with my uncle in san francisco,
eating good food and walking more miles

than I thought my legs could ever carry me;
my partner's first plane ride, the childlike wonder
as he watched our ascent from the window,
excitement growing as we rose into clouds;
how it felt to hold my sister for the first time;
how it felt to hold my brother for the first time;
how it felt to collect these memories,
to love with my entire being, to laugh, to cry
to live—

wildfire

on the 4th of july, neighbors light fireworks
within city limits.
not firecrackers, but the real kind,
exploding in dazzling displays of orange & white & green,
falling in shimmering embers. they cheer
and holler at the boom of gunpowder.
for weeks afterwards,
fireworks haunt the night and

all I think about is jasper, alberta,
half a town destroyed and acres of life burning to ash.
I think about the article I read two weeks ago,
how california's wildfires have burned
five times as much land this summer
than they have on average.
it's only july, and 178,000 acres and counting
burned from a single fire. I think
about the sun two nights ago,
scarlet and hazy in the smoke
drifting south from canada to the san juan islands,
summer's uninvited guest.

there's a stillness in a burnt forest.
if you drive into the north cascades,
you can find a section of corpses. trees uprooted;
others upright with blackened bark and bare of leaves.
birdsong exists as a distant melody;
no birds make their nests here.
there is no life in death. I find no beauty in flame.

ink

the pain is worst on the lowest part
of my wrist—I imagine the needle
puncturing bone, pinpricks of green and purple
staining my skeleton. permanent souvenirs:
sprig of lavender for me, floral bouquet for you,
to commemorate a weekend in the city.
we tell the artist we were girls together.
still young enough to play pretend,
to play kickball at recess. so long ago,
yet not long at all—not really.
we tell her how we kept in touch
after I moved away, and here we are.
old enough to get tattoos together in seattle.
we wrote letters: page after page
detailing our lives over months and years;
written record of our teenage years,
gathered in a box
and stored alongside childhood.
do you remember
how impossible life felt at fifteen?
diaries became letters became diaries
until ink dripped from cramping fingers,
smeared on the page. now ink dyes flesh,
pierces bone. another thing to bind us.

i
my life: marked by milestones
of meals, snapshots of snacks
shared over tables.
our house
was   is   always will be   the family home.

I can't imagine a time
when it won't be
but that time will come.

I wonder how many memories these walls
can hold. how many
birthdays, births, deaths, marriages, holidays, graduations
have been celebrated amongst
yellow wallpaper and floral couches.
we send everyone home with a plate

(or two)
(or three)

and still have two fridges stuffed with left
overs. my mother spends hours in the kitchen
with my aunt. they feed us   all.

we break bread; we tell stories. over cioppino,
my uncle laughs and shares an anecdote

(or two)
(or three)

about the east coast, about my grandparents,
about the time my cousins returned
home from camp to discover an empty
house, because he and auntie carole moved
while they were gone. we talk about her,
about aunt carole and aunt carmella
and noni and everyone who isn't with us
       anymore.
we lost people, but they live in every story,
in every cheesecake my mother bakes.

ii
in the house I grew
up in, my mother
       grew a garden; two barrels
       of herbs in the backyard—basil, parsley, over
flowing mint crowding the rest.

*   I remember*
*   planting beans one year,*
*   but they didn't make it.*

my mother has the green thumb
in the family—she only passed it to
my brother.

my grandpa has a garden, too, filled
with tomatoes and peppers and herbs and
in the front yard—apricots and accidental
pomelos. in the backyard is a menagerie

of fruits; apple trees lining the
pool, plums and peaches hugging
the concrete fence on the corner
of branham and snell, one large
and magnificent fig tree that holds
our tire swings and covers the yard in sticky sweet seeds.
the yard is as full of life as the home that
housed nine people at once.   three generations.

iii
often I wonder if I can carry on
this legacy, if I will be home for
                  my family
                            for my family's
                                          family

—I cannot grow things like my
grandpa or cook like my mother. I burn
batches of cookies and undercook
squash. but practice makes perfect.
my mother taught me to make a recipe
my own,
to mix part of myself into it.

so I am practicing—

eldest daughter

life lived in liminal space. nostalgia
as a state of being. the first to leave and
the first to miss it: the normalcy of it all,
the routine and responsibility that has built
the foundation of your life.
eldest daughters are practice
children, trailblazers
of discipline and achievement.
you are not a perfectionist
because you wish to be, but because
life requires perfection.
ask anyone and they will describe you as
punctual // obsessive // anxious.
you people-please, but write soliloquies in silence,
the things you'd say if you were brave enough.
you never say them.
you, eldest daughter, want peace.
you are a lover, not a fighter.
       inside you beats a heart comprised
       of infinite subsidiary chambers, small
       pockets for each soul you love,
       have ever loved. you carry the weight

of being the eldest,
of being a woman; you carry
generational trauma.
the eldest daughters before you
live in your spirit, and their grief is   heavy.
you fix and plan, and you weep
and laugh, and you give and give.
 above all else,
       you give.

seventeen

home is the house on 34th avenue
and I am seventeen, a high school senior.
my friends call me KATHY.
KATHY—the hard 'k' and the drawn out 'eee'
and the cacophony as it leaves the mouth.
I don't like it, I tell my friends. *I prefer kat.*
they don't listen. eventually, I give up,
stop asking them to call me something else.
I can't lose them. at seventeen, I am learning
how to navigate life and
my friends are learning with me—
we're all desperate for connection and
a little self-absorbed.
we compare scars and disordered eating
like notes, whisper secrets behind locker doors.
we all have something we fear,
and I fear being forgotten.
I turn to words: stories
handwritten in spiral-bound notebooks, poems
scrawled messily in the margins
of my homework. words will never leave me.
words will exist after I am gone, let no one forget me.
I begin to wonder: is life really worth living?
I watch my life like it belongs to someone else,
a ghost. my experiences
feel like memories in the moment,
faded and grainy. I don't know
who I am or who I want to be.
all I know is the intense pressure of
not-knowing. all I know
is my words will remain.

how to disappear

become a ghost that haunts the narrative. a presence
that is questioned. be there, but in the background:
anchor yourself to the wall, aerial roots puncturing
plaster until you are part of the room, until you are
the room itself; speak only when spoken to,
voice a whisper, like autumn leaves stirred
by light breeze, indiscernible from the sigh
of the building's bones. make yourself small, smaller,
until you cease to exist in corporeal form
and become a shadow, a phantom, an imprint.

until they question whether you were only ever
a fabrication, a wish that has since faded into nonbeing.
until they forget to remember you at all.

192
for alex

—that's how many days have passed since I learned you had left us. scrolling through facebook, your name appeared on my screen once, then again, and then I realized. when they said "alex," they meant you. you went to rehab and now I write poems in your memory. last year in british columbia: one thousand, seven hundred and sixteen people overdosed. including you. now you're a statistic, and I don't know what to do with my grief.

two days ago, I cried in the shower. spotify played "boulevard of broken dreams" and I thought of you. of the way you played guitar, singing your heart out in the stuffy school computer lab. how much time did we waste? seventeen and the rest of our lives ahead of us. I told you that you'd be famous someday. you told me to keep living, even when I didn't want to. I wish you took your own advice.

summer vacation

my grandfather calls on my twenty-sixth birthday,
asks me to visit—*one more summer at 168*, he says.

I'm thinking of selling the house, he says. I find
cheap flights online, book a rental car, buy a suitcase.

four months later, I fly to california with the love of my life
to spend one sentimental week revisiting my childhood.

it feels different & not-different all at once. the house
has been remodeled, but the air smells the same & the sun

is still hot & the fruit trees still grow. I find comfort
in the familiar: the sweet perfume of hot pink flowers blooming

from the bougainvillea; discordant traffic beyond
the yard, a mess of screeching tires and worn brakes;

hot pavement beneath bare feet; teeth tearing through the soft
flesh of ripe plums, sweet juice dripping down my chin;

one section of wall still bears old wallpaper, faded yellow
with blue flowers and dated penmarks where we grew;

in monterey, my grandmother joins us for a seaside picnic,
ocean spray kissing our faces. I find sadness in the absence:

the garden fence, torn down; the apricot tree, fallen down;
the yard too quiet without the dogs; my sister is not

in the bed next to mine, our brother is not down the hall.
there is loss that comes with growing & moving on & changing.

four years later, and my grandfather still lives in that house—
our house, the family house—and ghosts of childhood remain,

haunting me. oh, to be sixteen again for a day, for a summer.
what could I have done to keep things as they were?

anhedonia

in my most depressive episodes,
things I love lose their charm,
become chores in need of completion.
I feel no joy from activities
that used to bring pleasure.
this happens suddenly,
before I realize I no longer enjoy them.

let me tell you what I miss: dough
caked under fingernails and skin brittle
from handwashing and wrists sore from
kneading and mixing, the scent of cake
or spiced cookies, bread or berry pie
infusing the kitchen; the rustle of soft paper
as I turn page after page, consuming
stories with ferociousness, a new horror
in hardcover or the worn spine of a book
well-read in youth; the soothing scratch
of pen on paper, poems coming to life
amongst ink smears and coffee stains,
in which I write of
love & grief & other beautiful things.

late june

we swim against the current.
waves slam us against the pier;
bruised bodies, hands and feet
cut on clusters of barnacles, saltwater
swallowed as we struggle
to stay afloat. cramped muscles and
sore limbs until our feet touch
sand and pebbles as we reach the shore.

we sunbathe on the grassy hill
overlooking the water, sun setting
across the bay in a variegated sky.
we are on the brink of adulthood,
our lives ahead of us, but
adolescence exists fiercely in this moment
as damp skin & dripping hair. we soak
in laughter until the sky grows dark.

we say goodbye in tears. I thought
I could spare myself the heartbreak
of inevitable goodbyes and lost friends
by refusing to name this place home.
in my rejection, it burrowed itself
deeper into my heart, barbs hooked deep
into tissue. belongings in boxes and poems
in notebooks are all I have left.

twenty-one

home is a small island near the san juans.
I am twenty-one and bored.
if you've been to one small town,
you've been to them all.
everyone knows everyone and
I am an outsider. I don't belong
to this place. where do I fit in?
I keep to myself, keep busy—
I work part-time
brewing saturday-morning-coffee—
I take the bus out of town,
take community college classes—I write
poems in moleskin notebooks—
I start dating a bartender
a few years older than me and we drive
into the mountains, into the city,
anywhere but here, as far as we can get
for the day—I fall in love
for the first time and he starts to feel like home.
I don't know what to do
with that feeling. as a child,
I looked toward the future;
one day, I stopped
and I forgot to expect a life.
how do I start living now?

the ache that turned into art

I healed from it, you know;
the ache that turned into art.
the poems written in blood
that dripped from my wounds,
slowly / pouring / flooding.
the sculptures of broken bone
sharp and waiting to collapse.
the songs born of desperate,
howling cries—sobs rising
from the center of my soul.
I remain scarred, but healed,
surrounded by art
made from the pain of you.

when I long for you, I long for sundays
a poem as my grandmother

when I long for you, big brother, I long for sundays—how we skipped church and spent our mornings hiding in the laundromat smelling of mildew and damp socks—the one with the window covered in streaks and spiders—talking, laughing about nothing, until the day mom saw us sitting in front of the large window across the street from our house—mom was furious, but grandma laughed till she cried and begged her not to punish us—and how she stayed for dinner—and I don't remember what we had that night, but I remember waking up so early to the smell of tomato sauce simmering in the kitchen—dad standing at the stove, stirring, singing to himself—so it was probably spaghetti, and mom probably made banana cream pie (my favorite) or lemon meringue (your favorite)—and how if it wasn't spaghetti, it was crispy fried chicken and buttery potatoes—and how we never went hungry—even when all we had was ketchup and half a loaf of white bread—and how we spent nights listening to music together—how those little 45s echoed through the room—and some nights, mom played the piano by ear, not by book—and we hovered around her and sang along—and you knew every singer and the words to every song.

when I think of sundays, I think of you—how you were my whole world and how I was yours—best friend, big brother—and I think of how you were always fighting by my side—and when you weren't anymore I didn't know what to do or who I was or how to keep going—but I did—and finally I can listen to those 45s again and taste lemon meringue pie and do all the things we did together—because you're still here in my heart—and I know when I see you next—you'll be able to tell me the name of the song that starts to play when I see you again—

I wrote this poem as an offering

comfort has never
been comfortable for me.
I'm frightened by tears,
threatening to drown me
in a deep sea of salt water and pain.
my arms around your frame feel clunky,
heavy, and I worry you will break.
I'm sorry.
I don't know what to do.
let me, instead,
write you a poem
full of beauty & sadness & words
I would say if only I were stronger.
let me, instead,
write you a poem,
salve for the grieving heart.

rootbound

this morning, I found small tendrils creeping from
drainage holes—a sign my spider plant and her babies

need a bigger home. I don't wear gloves while I re-pot.
I like to feel the soil between my fingers, under my nails

imagine the damp earth seeping greedily into my skin,
helping me grow. the plant is rootbound and sturdy—

thick, tuberous roots cling to ceramic walls
and refuse to let go. I coax it out: tip the plant

on its side, loosen soil with delicate fingertips,
freeing it from its cage. there is dirt packed

in the crevices of the rootball and I take my time
untangling each root. I imagine it feels good to breathe,

to be noticed, to have someone care for you and tend
to you and realize you have outgrown your home.

> does anyone see the signs in me? my roots
> are wound too tight
> and my leaves are wilting.
> I long for someone to nurture me,
> find me a new home
> where I am not confined.

in which I compose a love letter

do you remember the way the mid-morning sun crept through the blinds of your basement apartment, the one I moved into that spring? so many days, I woke before you and admired the sunlight illuminating your face. I have memorized you: the sharp ridge of your nose, each hair on your face, your maple-syrup eyes. I could be away from you for centuries and never forget each detail. love has etched you onto my soul forever.

one morning, I looked at you and tried to remember the first time I said *I love you*—a lifetime of giving *I love you* and a lifetime of receiving it has clouded my memory. in that moment, I felt such guilt. should I remember? should this memory be as clear in my mind as your likeness?

maybe.

but I remember that day by the lake: my head on your shoulder under the warm spring sun. we rested after a hike, sore and sweaty. your voice echoed through the trees, rolled across the water, and I swear I could see ripples where your laugh skipped across the surface. in that moment, I realized I loved you. I have never stopped.

your laughter still shakes the water. we're still together in the sunlight.

twenty-three

home is a dorm apartment on bill mcdonald.
I am twenty-three and live with strangers
who become friends.
we stay up late, whisper in the dark
between lofted twin beds.
my days are filled with craft books and poems
drafted in melancholic numbness;
I write of happier times, I write of not being here.
when my roommates graduate, we buy
cheap vodka and get drunk in the living room.
we dance and laugh and—for a moment—
nothing matters. the early morning classes,
midterm flashcards, caffeine shakes.
it is us, just us.
and then it's over, just like that.
they move on, and I live with
different strangers who sleep all day
and let the trash can overflow.
I will never feel at home in this impermanence.
I weep when I am alone—for my family,
for comfort and order—I weep as I realize
that adulthood means I can never truly go home.

homecoming

orcas are sacred in the salish sea.
our southern residents, pride of
puget sound. to separate us
from them is impossible—even in guilt.
decades ago, violence
haunted our shores and penn cove
became a hunting ground.
young orcas captured; the drowned,
weighed down to the seabed.
tokitae was given
a new name
and captive life in a small pool
three thousand miles
from home. but
she remembered the ocean.
fifty-three years
of solitude, of calls home
echoing off concrete walls. she called
for her family in a language
only they know. confined to a life
of freedom as memory, her return
to ancestral waters promised
and unfulfilled.

after her death, her remains were returned,
scattered in the waters
of her birth, of what should have been her life.
a year later, the orcas returned
to penn cove for the first time
in fifty years. among them, ocean sun:
sole survivor

of her matriline, witness
to brutality.
maybe she shared this story
with her family, spoke the language
tokitae would have known.
did they feel her restored?
there is healing
in return, and wounds
that cannot heal. a life
of unanswered calls, homecoming
in death.

empty nest

to celebrate twenty-five years of marriage, my parents take a weekend trip. while they are gone, I return home. I pack my toiletries, and clothing for a few days; I bring books and journals, notebooks and pens. for four days, I care for the house, for the dogs and the cat. I drag the garbage and recycling bins to the curb the first night, bring them in the next afternoon. I wash dishes, straighten pillows on the couch. my clothes are covered in dog hair and my mind jumps at each moan of the settling house. each night, the cat sleeps by my side. this is not the first time I have looked after the house for my parents. this is the first time it has not felt like home.

my parents have tended an empty nest for eleven days. seven years since I left for college; last summer, my brother; last week, my sister left. we are gone now, my parents alone. the emptiness is palpable. this time, I sleep in my old room, the one my sister took when I left for college, pushing furniture through the door before the car had even left the driveway. the room is not bare. my brother's old bed, my sister's desk—these things remain, alongside photos on the wall and a contact lens on the bathroom floor. there are traces of my family, things left behind to haunt me.

as the first child to leave, the absence of my own belongings has never bothered me. the absence of my siblings, of their possessions, unsettles me, reminds me that time keeps moving and I cannot stop it. what I would give to rewind, to live in this house with my brother and sister again: my favorite gold ring, a bow covered in false diamonds; my books, stacked and overflowing from shelves; tumbled stones of ocean jasper, beloved gifts; handwritten letters from my best friend; the letter my parents wrote when I left, stored tenderly in my wallet. I would give my poems—all I have ever written and will ever write—to return to a life of togetherness, to be whole again.

autumnal shift

blink, miss it. green—gold—
gone—metamorphic rustle
of lives past, no more.

eyes on minneapolis
*for alex pretti, renee good, & every life
ruined and taken by ice*

saturday: I watch a public execution
before my first cup of coffee.
I watch masked federal agents
beat a man in minneapolis,
hear gunshots ring out as life ends
arbitrarily on the frozen sidewalk.

wednesday: I watch a masked agent
shoot a woman in the face, I see
her blood splattered on the headrest.
she is left, dying, aid refused
as her breathing stops and pulse slows.
I read her poem again and again.

tuesday: I watch a little boy, aged five,
with a spiderman backpack and teary eyes,
used as bait on his way home from school.
he and his father are detained, sent to texas.
they are here legally. he looks like
my nephew, also five, also latino.

friday: I watch twin city streets flood
in below zero temperatures,
thousands of people on strike.
the state closes as minnesota does
what minnesota does best: protests
injustice, murder, secret police.

everyday: from 1,730 miles away,
I watch minneapolis, under siege.
I watch my hometown fight back,
watch government-sanctioned
brutality against my city.
my heart breaks / my heart swells.

bloodlines
with sydnee smith

when I leave california, I take a lemon.
I inspect each one carefully, oblong orbs of daylight
hanging from heavy branches, nestled
among deep, evergreen leaves.
I need to pick the perfect one.

satsuma plums grow in rows against the back fence
of theresa's house in paradise,
their heavy branches bend over the pool.
the fruit ripens across the california desert
in august. my favorite time to visit. the plums
a blood moon hanging low enough to touch.

these are the sweetest lemons, grown in the backyard
of the truest home I have ever known.
I imagine roots sprawled for miles
under concrete, under soil. etching DNA
into earth for eternity.
time passes and things change: my grandfather
slows down; my grandmother's memory fails;
my great-uncle passes; but the lemons
never change. is this my family's legacy?

i visit every summer with my grandparents.
i spend the 2 hour car ride watching the fields;
the trees and vineyards paint colors across the window.
when we arrive everything is always as i remember.
i swim laps in the pool, competing with

                      my cousin to see who can hold their breath
                          the longest underwater. she always wins.

as children, we tossed lemons from the pool.
they fell from the branches, rolled
into the chlorinated water, floating as we swam.
we always threw them back to the earth.
as we aged, the tree leaned further, dropping more
lemons in our path.
(we never swim together anymore.
we never visit at the same time.)

               we emerge gasping, the thick air slapping our lungs.
               i throw my body over the edge of the pool and pluck
               a swelling plum. the first bite is the most satisfying.
                       the skin a bitter wall to break through
                         to the sweet flesh. the deep maroon juice
                                   spills down my chin.

my lemon makes the journey home.
809 miles, carried alongside books
and poems and other precious things.
I tenderly peel the coarse skin
from the fruit's flesh,
use my fingers to coax the seeds free.
        an act of labor / an act of love.
I rinse pulp from the seeds. bury them gently
in soil. if I am lucky, my own tree will grow.

                  i flash my teeth and say i am a vampire
                  and spit the seeds in a pile by the pool.

                    a ritual, an offering to the satsuma plums,
                      a prayer for their rebirth every august.
                    a prayer that i will be here to see them again.
                             (we never swim together anymore.
                                    we don't visit anymore.)

I think about change. about the passage of time.
about death.
I think about the way that nothing
remains the same forever, and how one day
the lemon tree in california may no longer exist.
will growing my own tree prevent this?
will my lemons taste as sweet?

                             the land was wiped clean one summer
                           in a fire that took everything from paradise.
                         the trees a discarded pile of ash. i don't even know
                             where they once grew. no plums will ever taste
                                   the same as theresa's paradise plums
                          and i will never return to the land with the plums
                                 and the pool and the seeds in the grass
                                       that weren't enough to offer.

twenty-four

home is my boyfriend's apartment
during the pandemic.
I celebrate my golden birthday and
three weeks later the entire world stops.
I struggle with the change.
he lets me hang lights from the ceiling,
line the windows with houseplants,
graciously clutter his room
with hastily-packed belongings.
six homes later and I'm still not sure
what should remain packed, when to feel settled.
the days blur together:
he plays video games
while I take college classes
in bed, books stacked on sheets;
I box-dye my hair, lose my job,
lose my friends, get wine drunk too often.
I pick up a pen and start writing, searching
for solace within our solitude. poetry
provides comfort, escape—but briefly.
each day mirrors the last,
a never-ending cycle of fear and
apathy and outrage and grief.
it is at twenty-four that I learn loneliness
can break you. maybe
beyond repair.

pandemic poem for my mother

I want to write a poem
for my mother, but how
do I write of her eyes—the way
they shimmer like golden
pendants in the california sun.
how can words describe
her voice and how it sounds like
home, is home.
because she has made every
empty house feel like a home.
I can't find a way to write
of her baking, of how
the kitchen smells like love
& sugar, because no metaphor
compares to the taste
of early morning scones
and I remember the cake
she baked when I left for college,
and how much I missed her
that first week, and
I miss her even more
now. how can I write
anything at all
when words
typed on an 8x11 sheet of paper
are just that—words, not
my mother. not
home.

drop

if you asked me what grief feels like,
I'd tell you to imagine driving
through the mountains.
the road curves gently
through the base of a towering mountain range,
slopes littered
with cedars and subalpine firs;
huckleberry shrubs or wildflowers,
depending on the season.
the leaves might be green, or gone,
maybe the vibrant orange of autumn.
unimportant:
the colors, the season.
important: the beauty, the serenity.

without warning, the road ends
and there is a great nothingness
beyond you. you fall into the void
and cannot see the bottom.
will you fall forever?
the slopes and their trees
pass in a blur of greens and browns,
but you fall as if through sap—slow
and suffocating.

and then there you are,
back on the road. pavement beneath
rubber, hands on the wheel, in the car.
the road is the same again—mountain peaks stretching
towards clouds, trees and shrubbery distinct.
that terrifying drop towards the void just a bad dream,
easy to forget—until it returns. you turn left

when you should have turned right
and you're falling again,
down
        down
                down
and think, *this is it, I'll hit the end soon*,
but you don't. you are safe on solid ground.

this falling happens again and again
and again. you notice
each drop is shorter. there is momentary peace
and the moments grow longer, give false hope
of permanence.
you drive through the mountains, admire
beauty through a lens of fear. you don't know when
you'll fall again, but you know you will.

elegy for an unborn daughter

in my dreams, I have a daughter. she has my smile, warm and stretching across her cheeks like it will burst. she has her father's eyes—soft and gentle—and his laugh. she is perfect. I give her a beautiful name, and she is everything I wish for her to be. she is curious, always asks questions and tries new things and lives without my fear of failure; she is generous, never selfish, but builds firm boundaries; she shows kindness to each soul she meets. I teach her everything my parents taught me. she learns how to read, to escape into a story and to write her own. she learns how to proof a loaf of bread, how to cut butter into flour and dust berries in flour before adding them to batter. she learns how to love, how to be loved. her life is beautiful, free from worry and filled with joy.

only in my dreams do I have a daughter. she deserves freedom, but I cannot give her freedom. I know the life that awaits her. to be expected to give and give and give and give and give and give. to provide with every facet of her being; labor that is physical, emotional, mental, financial. to set her dreams aside for someone else's, to be happy about that, to be willing to pretend to be happy about that. she deserves safety, but I cannot keep her safe in this life. a life where she is little more than prey to someone else: the man at the bar, the boy with the gun. I would teach her everything life taught me—keys between knuckles and block the door and hide away from windows and never rent on the first floor and never walk with headphones on and learn self-defense, because boys will be boys will be monsters—but what life is a life lived in fear? I long to hold her in my arms, but she is safer in my heart. so there she will stay.

strange survivor's guilt

each day: a new anger,
a new sadness, another injustice.
men and women and children
    starving / sick / hunted
    / dying.
gratitude feels heavier this year.
food on my table, my family safe
and healthy. why
should anyone else know differently?
I do not pray,
but I pray for what I have,
that I do not lose it. I ask forgiveness
for my fortune, strange
survivor's guilt over what I have to feel
thankful for. a life lived in.
comfortability
like this is coveted—not wealth
or power, but without fear of loss.
a life lived in
fear is no life at all.
somehow, I am still living.

the summer joel miller died

my doctor doesn't know what's wrong with me.
she orders a blood test, an x-ray; she refers me
to a specialist who runs more tests.
an MRI shows something, he can't tell what.
all I see is a dark smudge in my tissue.
something is wrong. my foot swells to two,
three, four times its size—the muscle feels
as though it's being
s t r e t c h e d
and I can't move my toes. I can't go home.
for months, my parents examine photos
of the bruised and swollen extremity
and they—in their infinite
parental wisdom—are lost.
they cannot heal me, cannot kiss it better
or slap a bandaid on it or run my skin
under cool water the way they did
when I touched a lightbulb at five.
I want answers and no one has them.
not you, not my parents, not me—
and it's my own foot.
the specialist schedules exploratory surgery.

no one is allowed with me in the clinic,
because no one is allowed anywhere right now.
I check in alone, look away
as the anesthesiologist hooks me up to the IV.
the anxiety pill doesn't work.
the soft cloth mask over my mouth and nose
makes my anxiety worse,
serves as a reminder that I am here alone
and my parents aren't here and

you aren't here and maybe I'm not even here.
I lie down in a blue operating room, sterile
and cold both in physicality and feeling,
and open my eyes again in a recovery cubicle
with bar-lighting—dim, yellow.
nurses dart in and out from the thin curtain
as I try to remember when I closed my eyes,
whether there was music playing in the OR
or maybe I'm thinking of my wisdom teeth,
because I don't remember closing my eyes,
but the nurses are telling me it's over,
it's time to get dressed and go home.
they help me into my clothing and wheel me out,
and I am placed—gently—into the car.

I don't remember much about the first day:
in and out of sleep and I keep dreaming
that joel miller is dead,
my foot numb in between naps until pain
wakes me, radiating from the ball of my foot.
you tend to me, pausing a video game
when I need food/water/medication.
I imagine my foot as a weather map, the pain
growing larger and intensifying
like a snowstorm or hurricane.
I can't wait for my next dose of painkillers.
when I am finally lucid, I say,
I had a dream that joel died,
and you say, *he did.*
he was beaten to death with a golf club.
I ask you to call for a refill on my painkillers.
a chunk of tissue carved from me, but
only a day's worth of oxycodone.
I want to shower—sweat clings to me
like a second skin, but I can't shower yet.

I want to eat—hunger claws at me,
but the pain unsettles my stomach.
I want fresh air—the room is stale,
but the wound is too fresh to attempt stairs.
I want my parents—I feel so alone
without them, though I am not alone,
and they are too far and we are quarantined.
my life is a paradox: I begin to heal while I lose
everything but you.

finally, I have stitches removed and ask the specialist,
what was it? what did you find
in the tissue you removed?
I expect an answer, definitive,
the way you answered me
when you told me I was not dreaming and
was actually awake long enough to watch joel die.
the specialist says, *we don't know.*
we found something in the soft tissue,
but whatever it was,
it was too disintegrated to identify.
and like that, I am left with no answers.
there will be no comfort in the isolation,
no consolation in the healing.
the tissue will proliferate,
my independence will return—slowly.
it could have been anything,
I guess: a shard of glass, a sliver
of wood, a cactus spike, a shattered fragment
of joel miller's skull.
it doesn't really matter now, I guess.
we all die someday, and loneliness
is the slowest death of all.

twenty-six

home is a small apartment in happy valley;
twenty-six and I feel lost.
I am closer to thirty
than I am to twenty. no one tells you
how much of your twenties
is spent figuring out who you are.
who am I? the world revived,
but I cannot find my place in it.
I tell my father it feels like time
moves parallel to itself, too fast and too slow
all at once. he says this
is the state of adulthood.
my best friend says this
is the cost of losing our mid-twenties to a virus.
I write poetry to solve the riddle of myself—
actually, the poems write themselves, but
they are missing something.
a sense of self, a sense of purpose?
if I knew, I wouldn't write with such urgency.
life will continue—but I wonder
if I have missed the chance to discover
meaning in my life? will I ever create something
more than empty poems?
will I ever feel at home in myself?

unofficial list of grievances

that there is not enough time in the day
for everything I wish to do,
like cook elaborate meals and bake cakes
and read every book I own
and write every poem in my heart
and take walks and listen to records and soak
in the tub and sleep in and journal;
that work consumes so much
of my time and so much of my energy;
that I must work at all, when I was meant
to forage for berries and mushrooms,
and listen to creeks and birds, and rot
on the forest floor; that I cannot live
forever, because one life is not long enough
to see every film and read every book
and travel to every place I dream of;
that I am alive at all, because
I never asked for sorrow or a whimsical soul;
that my best friend lives so far from me
and I cannot see her whenever I please
or laugh with her or cry on her shoulder
or exist in her presence for just a moment;
that dogs and cats do not live forever,
so I will always face inevitable heart/break
but will be there in their final moments,
whenever I can; that my parents will age,
rather than live forever, because who else
will understand everything I am
and everything I could be, love me and teach me
and wish happiness into my life like they have;
that it gets colder each december
and I cannot enjoy the snow; that it gets hotter

each june and I cannot enjoy the sun;
that my brain does not work, does not make
enough serotonin or dopamine on its own, so
I cannot enjoy much of anything;
that I will never again know my brother or sister
the way I did at eleven–fifteen–twenty–so fully
and truly, that our lives will forever be shared
in fragments; that my grandmother
cannot remember my age
and that I will never hear my uncle's laugh
again and that I no longer speak
to so many best friends I once loved deeply;
that I feel so much,
I wish sometimes I could not feel at all;
that I have not known the man I love all his life,
because that means there were years
I could not love him
and protect him as fiercely as I do now—

willow

my cat overgrooms—a bald spot
on her side, an inch in diameter,
that grows back until she licks it clean
again. I ask the vet: *neurotic*.

I worry constantly. like mother,
like daughter. the cat I adopted
for emotional support has inherited
my anxiety—a learned behavior

no different than biting my fingernails
or running my tongue across the edges
of my teeth till it bleeds, till it hurts.
I think about nature versus nurture—this,

of course, would be nurture, but
may be nature, since she was a stray
before she was a housecat,
and then I start thinking about

neuroticism as an inherited trait and how
I am, undoubtedly, a little neurotic,
but I wouldn't say the same of my parents,
so where did it originate in me? and how

do I un-neuroticize my cat? I listen
to her groom, licking licking licking
licking licking—and if it is my fault,
I want to take it from her.

denali

everything is grander in alaska—mountain
ranges taller and rivers wider and
early-autumn trees richer in color.
we walk a mile along the savage river,
cross a narrow bridge at trail's end.
the river's roar deafens us, muffles
all sound. water collides against boulders
of quartz and schist—violent, vibrant.
as we hike, my brother names flora and fauna;
plentiful fireweed and white-barked birch
trees, edible mushrooms, bright orange berries;
the magpie perched on a rock and
a ground squirrel emerging from the dirt.
his knowledge amazes me. it always has, but here,
he is more an adult than he has ever been at home.
on our way out, we pull off the road
to watch three grizzlies roam tall grass,
the alaska range beyond them stretching
into the clouds.

my brother seems disinterested. it occurs to me then
that he has seen wild grizzlies
before. he has traveled to the arctic circle,
has lived lives unimaginable
to me. he is brave enough to live here,
two thousand miles from home.
I took him camping the summer before he left.
we laid in the tent, washington rain battering
canvas as we shared childhood memories.
it was the first time I realized he was old enough
for nostalgia. but while I longed

for the comfort of our youth,
he was looking back
to move forward, into his life.

snowfall

tonight is cold. curled up
beneath a heavy blanket, cup of cocoa
warming my fingers, I joke
about being washingtonian.
he replies, *but you aren't really
from here.* that's true—I was
not born to the cascades, to midnight coyote
howls and puget sound rainstorms.
this is not who I am, but who I am
becoming.

I was born to the land of ten thousand lakes,
frozen over
on the day of my birth. I was born
in february, twenty-two days after
the coldest day recorded in minnesota history,
sixty degrees below zero.
that is my heritage, my legacy: bones of ice
and snowflake skin, poetry
piled high like last night's snowfall.
I cannot escape it.

it snowed this year in washington,
and the year before. maybe
that is why this place feels so familiar, why
I finally feel like I am from somewhere instead of
nowhere.
I stood, arms outstretched, under
a sky that opened up to remind me
of mittens clipped to coats, sleds and snowball fights.

I caught snowflakes on my tongue, waited
for sharp edges to pierce me—

but they didn't. they melted into me,
welcomed me home.

on seeing the aurora borealis

the first beautiful thing I see with new eyes
is the aurora borealis.
I bring eye drops to the park,
administer them in the car.
four days post-op, corneas healing,
my vision still blurs at night, artificial light
streaking across darkness like brushstrokes.
      the last time I saw this
      clearly, I was a child.
      I am hungry
      to see the world anew.
I see the aurora now—faint, but
there—I see it with the naked eye.
the night sky above the islands painted
green and purple, the sea a mirror
reflecting muted colors back to the moon.
never have I seen something so beautiful.
I don't believe in heaven; if it exists,
I imagine it looks like this.
in a single lifetime, we take
so much for granted: quiet evenings,
sturdy legs, sight without correction.
there is beauty in more than colorful skies
and deep blue seas, if you are willing
to see it.

twenty-seven

home is the island I swore I'd never return to,
and life is comfortable at twenty-seven:
brand new apartment, center of town;
degrees hung on the wall; dinners
with my family, with his family;
talk of marriage; travel and hiking and
day trips to the city.
but discomfort lurks beneath my skin,
sows seeds of unrest. what does it mean
if I settle down? settle here—or anywhere.
I might lose myself.
I've always had another home
on the horizon, had the comfort
of searching for myself in the next place.
poem after poem
after therapy session
and I still don't know who I am.
if I stay here, I might never find an answer.
I keep one box of things, precious keepsakes,
packed away and tucked
under the bed—just in case.

elegies for a small town

1

call me dramatic / I think I'll die if I stay here / by which I mean, I've burnt every bridge with a sharp tongue / by which I mean, I stopped tolerating small people / by which I mean, my therapist says that boundaries are uncomfortable for everyone but necessary for all / by which I mean, I am not crazy / by which I mean, my home is my sanctuary / by which I mean, get the fuck out / by which I mean, your breath stinks of cheap booze / by which I mean, it's pathetic to get drunk at 2pm / by which I mean, it's pathetic to get drunk every day / by which I mean, I stop drinking so I will never become them

2

another body. this place collects them like butterflies, dried and pinned to the fabric of small-town anguish. people are born to die young here, drowning in generational trauma. I hear the stories, attend the memorials. my heart aches. how do you process grief when loss doesn't stop?

3

no one talks to anyone / they talk behind backs, behind bars / hurl accusations / apologies never come / from conspiratorial tongues / my therapist says that intent means nothing, impact means everything / when he calls me a thief / he calls me your girlfriend / over and over / your girlfriend / your girlfriend / they all do / as if I am nothing but an appendage that begs / removing / I resent you for this, sometimes / I want to be the villain / I want to tear flesh from limb with my words alone / I want to bare my teeth, pomegranate juice dripping bloodlike from feral lips / I want to watch it all burn and rise / from the ashes

4

happiness doesn't live here: I have searched for it in the trees atop glacial mountains, at the bottom of bottles. don't you understand – this happiness only comes with a sugared rim. don't you understand – I am living the wrong life. I want to write of home. instead I write elegies for a place I cannot love.

5

passive-aggression as a sign I'm doing something right / by which I mean, I feel so lonely / it doesn't count as crying if salt tears run with shower droplets / I wish I could feel at home; I am adrift / I lash out to steady myself and instead find you / my therapist says that for every negative thing, you need five positives to balance it / so I leave water for you beside the bed each morning / an offering to offset harsh words / it is not your fault I am rootless

return to olympus

we must be a sight: cheeks wet
with tears, full-body sobs
as we sink to our knees on grass,
on gravel, my faded college sweatshirt
coated in white fur.
we are a family in mourning
and I've got a feeling
that the people next door
are used to this. I hope so.
I have sat in this very parking lot,
watched a couple enter with a dog
and exit alone, and I wept with them.
here I am now, after
one last walk, one last kiss,
one last *good girl*.
my father comforts me.
my father comforts my sister.
in our grief, we offer little comfort back,
and if this bothers him,
he doesn't say. he simply holds us.
we say little. we say our goodbyes.
athena, named before us,
named for the goddess of wisdom,
returns to olympus, or heaven,
or the stars, or wherever we go after.
I hope she felt how lucky we were
to love her, if only briefly.
I hope we loved her enough
to mend any old wounds.
I hope death is kind
to sweet girls.

girlhood

in adulthood, you'll be surrounded by women
who show you true girlhood—love,
administered as rituals of friendship:
a two-person book club with a college friend,
a poet who writes breathtaking poems,
who has the kindest soul and a passionate dislike
of bad writing and stupidity;
brunch dates with an old coworker,
the one from your first job, your first friend
in a new place who became your closest friend,
a permanent fixture in your life;
the woman you trade places with,
claiming washington as your home
while she adopts minnesota as hers,
who visits for good drinks and long talks;
irregular video calls and constant texts
with your best friend, the girl you met at eleven,
almost twenty years ago, who lives further
than you can bear, but knows you best of all;
your sister, if you are lucky enough to have one,
will be a woman you admire, a woman you miss
every moment you're apart, unexpected
after years of arguments and borrowed clothing.

you will savor each moment with all of them
and love them with every part of your soul.
they will show you love, in its truest forms.

trillium falls

the redwoods stand tall as the mountains
back home. they start small, skinny
trunks of murky bark; further along the trail,
they become giants, wide and red
and neverending. we take our time
on the trail, marvel that something
so ordinary could be so magnificent.
when we finally reach the falls,
you stand on roots wider than yourself,
snaking through each other
in a tangle of ancient bark.
I cannot tell how many trees make this knot.
trillium falls trickles slowly, gently,
into a creek of mossy stones
and we are alone
on the trail, just us and the birds
and the redwoods.
when I turn around, there you are—
kneeling before me, arms outstretched,
the ring box delicately cradled in your palms.
I sense your nervousness, see it
in your eyes and the deep inhale
before you ask me to marry you,
the towering trees as our witness.
I say yes—of course I say yes—kiss you
in the cool damp of the forest,
intertwined fingers
mirroring the roots beneath our feet.
we linger here, anchored
in the earth for as long as possible,
the redwoods no longer
the most beautiful sight I have seen.

driving past ghosts
after Noah Kahan's "The View Between Villages (Extended)"

do not speak to me of loss. you can grieve
so much more than you think—
and I grieve it all. fields in the valley
fill with ghosts: the best friends
of my youth, of my teenaged years,
now memories of girlhood; the songs
I loved and lived in
like favorite sweaters; the scars
and stretch marks on a body unloved;
a lap without cats, the silence
when I walk through a door
and dogs don't bark;
the meals uneaten and clothes
unworn and books unread;
the dreams I never followed; the homes
left behind and the pieces of me
left with them; the life I could have
lived
had I been whole.

they haunt me now, apparitions
of regret. my life
may not be long, but I want it to be full.
afraid not of death, but of dying
homesick for myself.

thirty

there is stillness in my life. I am thirty
and writing and married and childfree and
fulfilled. happiness and peace—the peace of
having found what I was searching for.

I never knew how to answer when you asked
about my hometown. I used to think home
was a fixed point, a set of coordinates on a map.
all I ever wanted was to belong to someplace.

home is the house I grew up in
(and the house after that (and the house
after that (and the house after that).
it is my sister's first steps, my brother's

first words. it is my mother's laugh,
my father's aftershave. it is my best friend's
floral-stained skin, and my cat's
soft snores from the foot of the bed.

it is my husband's gentle embrace, an occasional
weekend snowfall. it is midwest thunderstorms
and california heat and rainy nights
in the pacific northwest. it is every poem

I write and pour myself into. it is the return
of the orcas and distant grizzlies and the
acceptance of aging, of change. everywhere
I have been has led me here, to myself.

I am finally home.

notes & acknowledgements

I have so many people to thank.

dad, for believing in me. every book you've recommended, every poem you've read, each word of encouragement and reminder to keep writing—it's all led me here. I hope you always want to read the next thing. I hope I always make you proud.

mom, for teaching me that home isn't a place, but a feeling. for loving me. I could write a thousand poems and it still wouldn't be enough to accurately convey how grateful I am to have you in my life.

gabriella and anthony, for inspiring me. it's been such a pleasure to watch you both grow up and I admire both of you more than you'll ever know. thank you for being the best part of (most of) my life.

tre, for believing in me. for introducing me as a poet and for reading every poem. for being my best friend and the love of my life and my husband. I love you so much.

uncle dan, zizi, uncle kamake, grammy, grampy, uncle tony, aunt wendy, grandma terry, grandpa jim, my aunts & uncles, cousins & second cousins—for supporting me. whether you read my poetry, or have been the subject of my poetry, or have just loved me. thank you.

sydnee, for writing "bloodlines" with me, and for letting me include it in this book. you are one of my closest friends & favorite poets. writing a poem with you was a dream come true!!

cindy, for being my best friend for almost twenty years. I am beyond thankful for you. you're my platonic soulmate and I love u 4ever <3

becca, for being my first friend in anacortes (and the only competent employee at kfc/taco bell) and my forever brunch date.

lillian, for being the sweetest friend. I miss you every day, but I'm so thankful for every moment we spend together.

thank you to the following literary journals, where these poems were first published:
- the bitchin' kitsch (all my relations): "when I long for you, I long for sundays"
- sledgehammer lit: "what we leave behind"
- jeopardy magazine: "168"
- anti-heroin chic: "192"
- southchild lit: "on feeling lightning"

"the mountain is out" was written after Michelle Awad's prompt, "*have you listened to the mountains lately?*" (@theconstantpoet)

"things I'm afraid I'll forget with age" was written after Thea's prompt, "*things I'm afraid I'll forget with age*" (@lettersfrrompersephone)

"the ache that turned into art" was written after Shakun Sharma's prompt, "*the ache that turned into art*" (@thesubduedwords)

"I wrote this poem as an offering" was written after Zoë Lawrie's prompt, "*salve for the grieving heart*" (@zoelawriewriter)

"in which I compose a love letter" was originally published in my micro-chapbook, *from me, to you* (2023)

"strange survivor's guilt" was written after Thalia Clem's prompt, "*gratitude feels heavier this year*" (@authorthaliaclem)

"the summer joel miller died" was inspired, in part, by *The Last of Us Part II*, by Naughty Dog and Sony Entertainment.

"unofficial list of grievances" was written after Michelle Awad's prompt, "*unofficial list of grievances*" (@theconstantpoet)

"return to olympus" was written after Malachy Moran's prompt, "*and I've got a feeling that the people next door*" (@malformedpoetry)

"girlhood" was written after M. L MacDonald's prompt, "*love, administered*" (@ml_macdonald)

"driving past ghosts" was written after Noah Kahan's *The View Between Villages (Extended)*.

the following pieces were originally published on my substack, *fragments from a soft life*:
- "empty nest"
- "homecoming"
- "trillium falls"
- "girlhood"

the following pieces were originally published on vocal media:
- "how to disappear"
- "elegy for an unborn daughter"
- "autumnal shift"
- "drop"
- "elegies for a small town"

Katherine J Zumpano is a poet and writer in the Pacific Northwest. She graduated from Western Washington University in 2021, with a Bachelor of Arts in English, with a creative writing emphasis. Her debut poetry collection, *from me, to you*, was released in 2023. She has had poems published in several literary magazines, including Southchild Lit, Jeopardy Magazine, and WhatcomWRITES. She self-publishes poetry, essays, and short fiction on her Substack, *fragments from a soft life*.

Katherine lives with her husband and their cat, Willow, who supervises all writing sessions by napping as close to the keyboard as possible. For more poems, stories, and cat photos, you can follow her on Instagram and Threads @kjzwrites.

www.ingramcontent.com/pod-product-compliance
Ingram Content Group UK Ltd.
Pitfield, Milton Keynes, MK11 3LW, UK
UKHW022236230426
12048UKWH00018BA/1288